Collins

Cursive WRITING

FOUNDATION LEVEL 1

Published by Collins Learning
A division of HarperCollins*Publishers*
India Private Limited

Harper Collins Publishers
A-75, Sector 57, Noida,
Uttar Pradesh 201301, India

1 London Bridge Street, London, SE1 9GF,
United Kingdom

2 Bloor Street East, Toronto, Ontario M4W
1A8, Canada

Lvl 13, 201 Elizabeth Street (PO Box A565,
NSW, 1235), Sydney NSW 2000, Australia

195 Broadway, New York, NY 10007, USA

Browse the complete Collins catalogue at
www.collins.in
For any queries/feedback, please write to us
at **SCHOOLSUPPORT@harpercollins.co.in** or
call us on **0120-4044800**.

First published in 2020

Reprint: 10 9 8 7 6 5 4 3 2 1

ISBN: 978-935357-125-2

Artwork and layout by
Typeface Printographics Pvt. Ltd.

Printed and bound by
MicroPrints India, New Delhi

Acknowledgements

Cover: HarperCollins*Publishers*India

Title Page: HarperCollins*Publishers*India

Prelim Pages: yayayoy, tigatelu, TopVectors, musri, bruno1998

Preface

Writing, or forming letters by hand, creates a connection with the movement of the hand (fine motor skill) to the visual response of seeing the letter on the page (visual and tactile skills). It involves multiple processes that happen simultaneously: the movement of the hand, the thought of the letter, and the visual cue of the letter. As children grow older, the writing process combines both low-level skills—such as handwriting, spelling, and grammar—and high-level skills—organization, strategy, considering the parameters of the topic and the needs of the reader, etc. This is reading and writing concurrently, which is a necessary skill.

Although writing can be demanding to learn, it teaches organization skills and assists children in composing their own thoughts and ideas.

Benefits of Learning the Cursive Script

- Cursive writing helps train the brain to integrate visual and tactile information, and fine motor dexterity.
- Cursive has the added benefit of being both artistic and highly personal.
- Learning cursive handwriting is important for spelling skills, enabling children to recognize words when they read them later.
- For those struggling with dyslexia, cursive can a part of a remediation plan to help hand-eye coordination, memory, visual discrimination, and other brain activities.
- Practising writing in cursive is an important part of a curriculum that improves children's cognitive and visual skills.

Collins *Cursive Writing* is a three-book series that introduces children in the age group of 3—6 years to the cursive script in a carefully graded, age-appropriate manner. A lot of attention has been paid to the letter formations taught in this series. Unnecessary loops and flourishes have been eliminated. Starting dots and tracing lines have been included to facilitate the learning process.

Actual writing is not recommended for the first level. Instead, a variety of tracing and colouring activities are given to help children develop their grip—the ability to hold a pencil and develop motor memory.

Loops and patterns are introduced in the second level. This is followed by introduction to the cursive formation of small letters. In keeping with the overall level of learning for this level, the writing of words is introduced at the end of the second level.

The writing of capital letters in the cursive script is covered in the third level. This level concludes with the tracing/writing of complete sentences, which is a useful skill for children entering primary school.

Contents

This book belongs to:

Let's Have Fun

Scribble on the big fat hen with crayons.

Let's Trace Patterns

Trace the patterns.

Let's Trace Patterns

Trace the patterns.

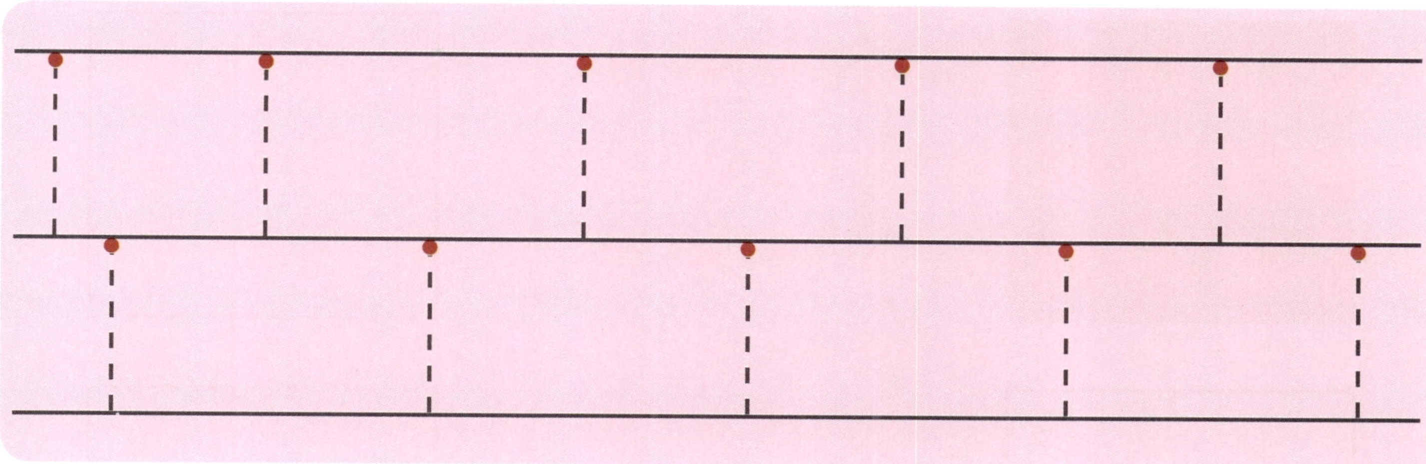

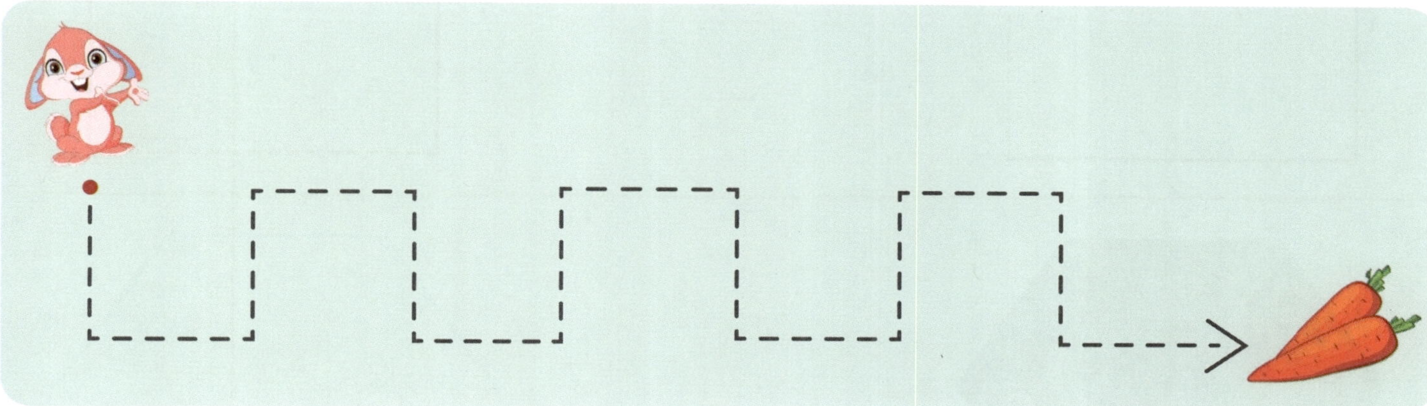

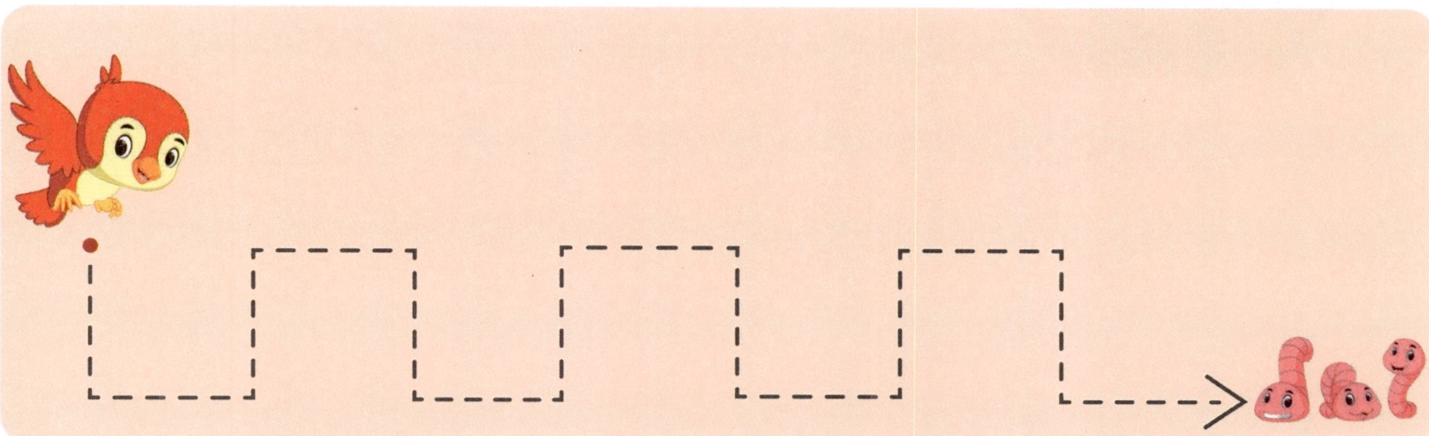

Let's Get Ready

Trace and complete the picture. Colour it.

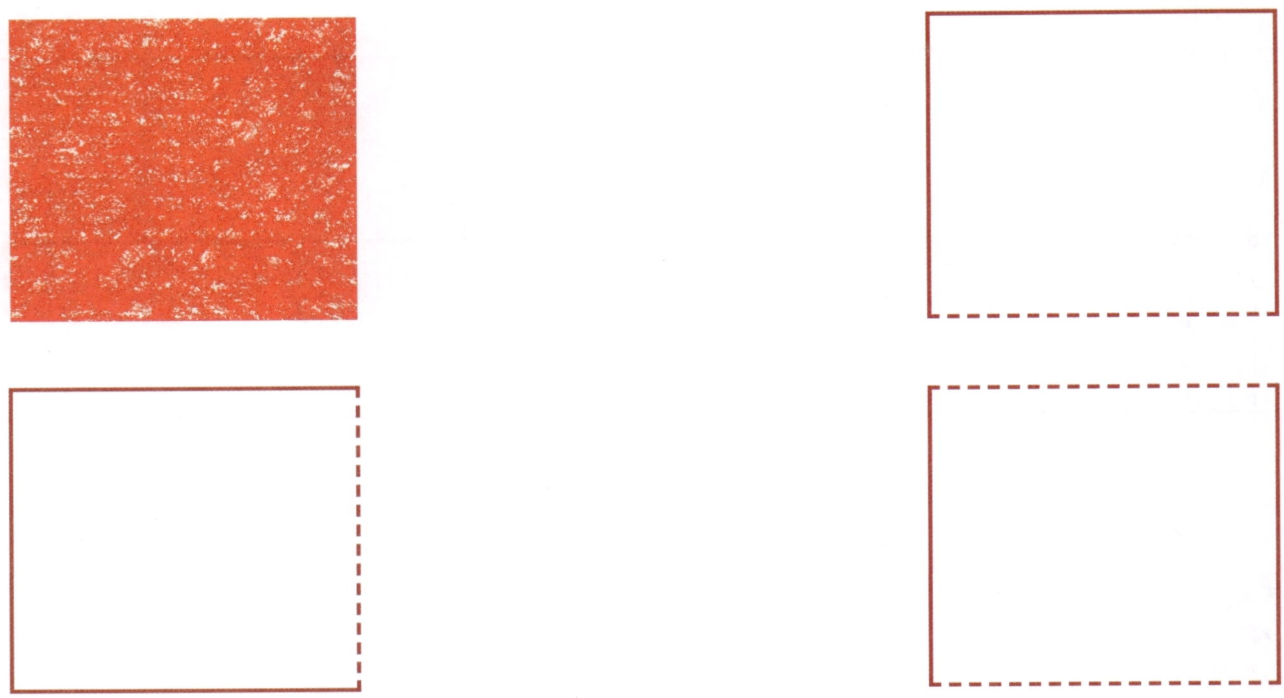

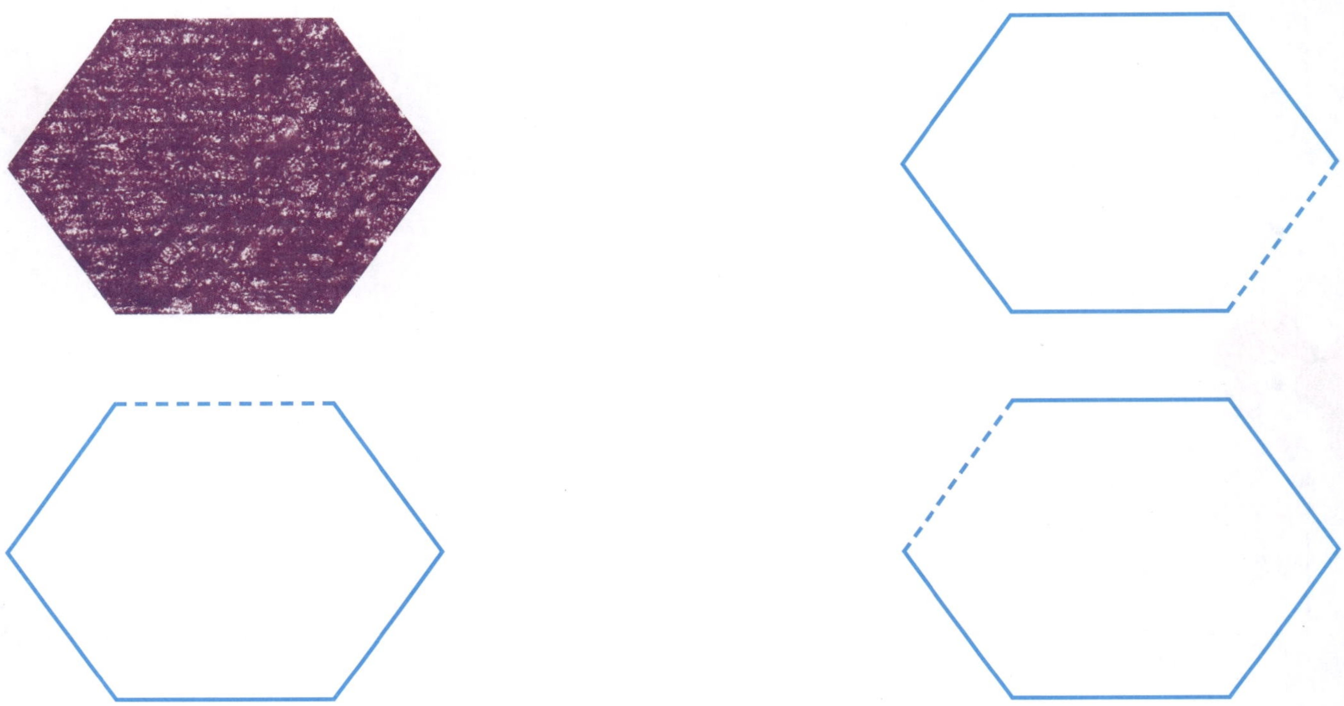

Let's Get Ready

Trace and complete the picture. Colour it.

Let's Get Ready

Trace and complete the picture. Colour it.

Let's Get Ready

Trace and complete the picture. Colour it.

Let's Get Ready

Trace and complete the picture. Colour it.

Let's Trace Patterns

Trace the patterns.

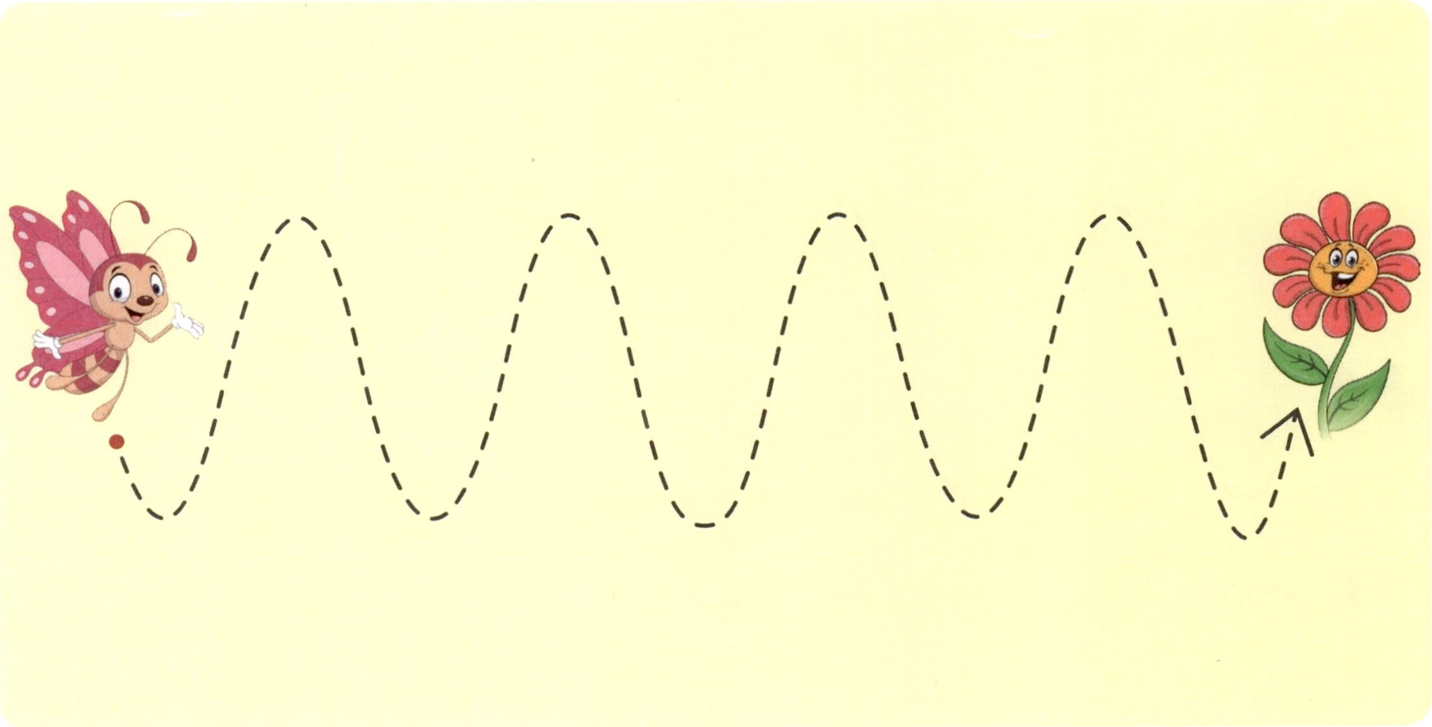

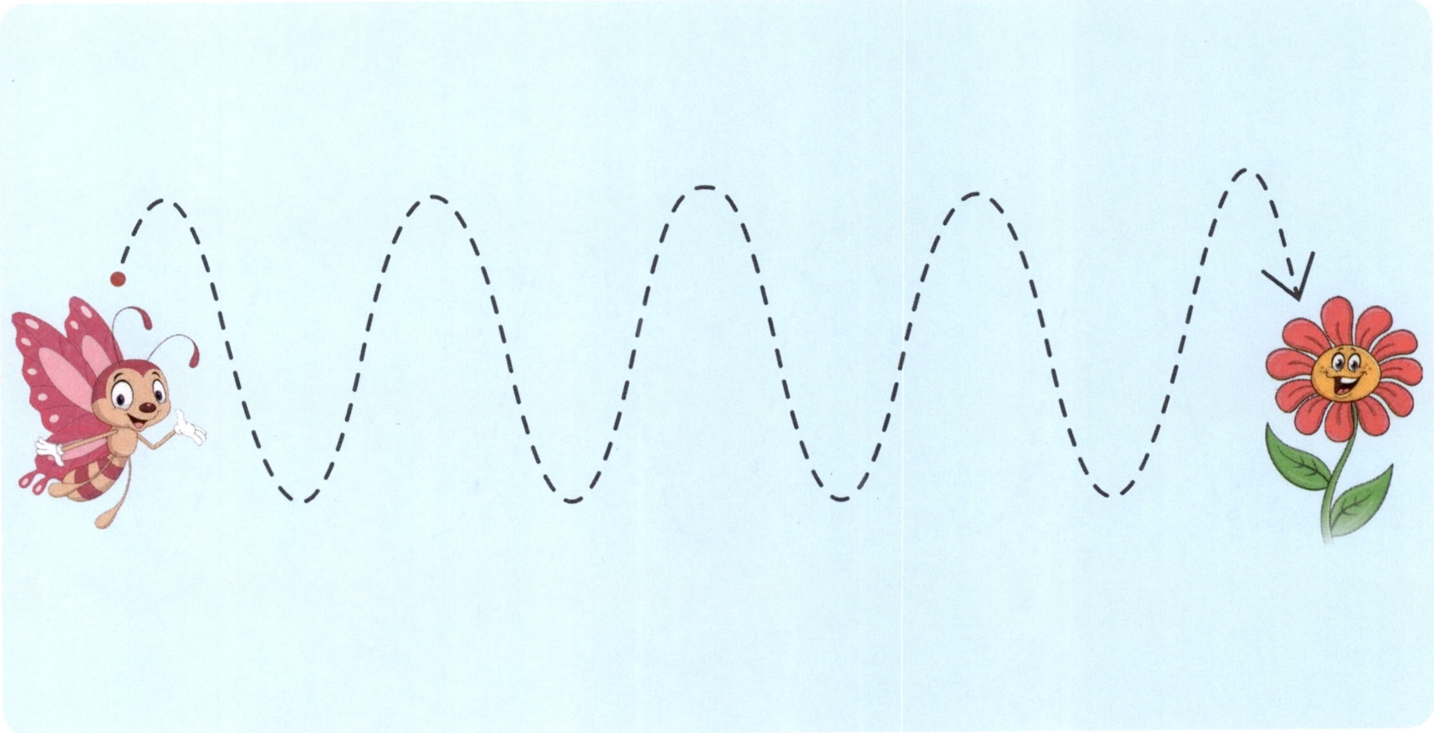

Let's Trace Patterns

Trace the patterns.

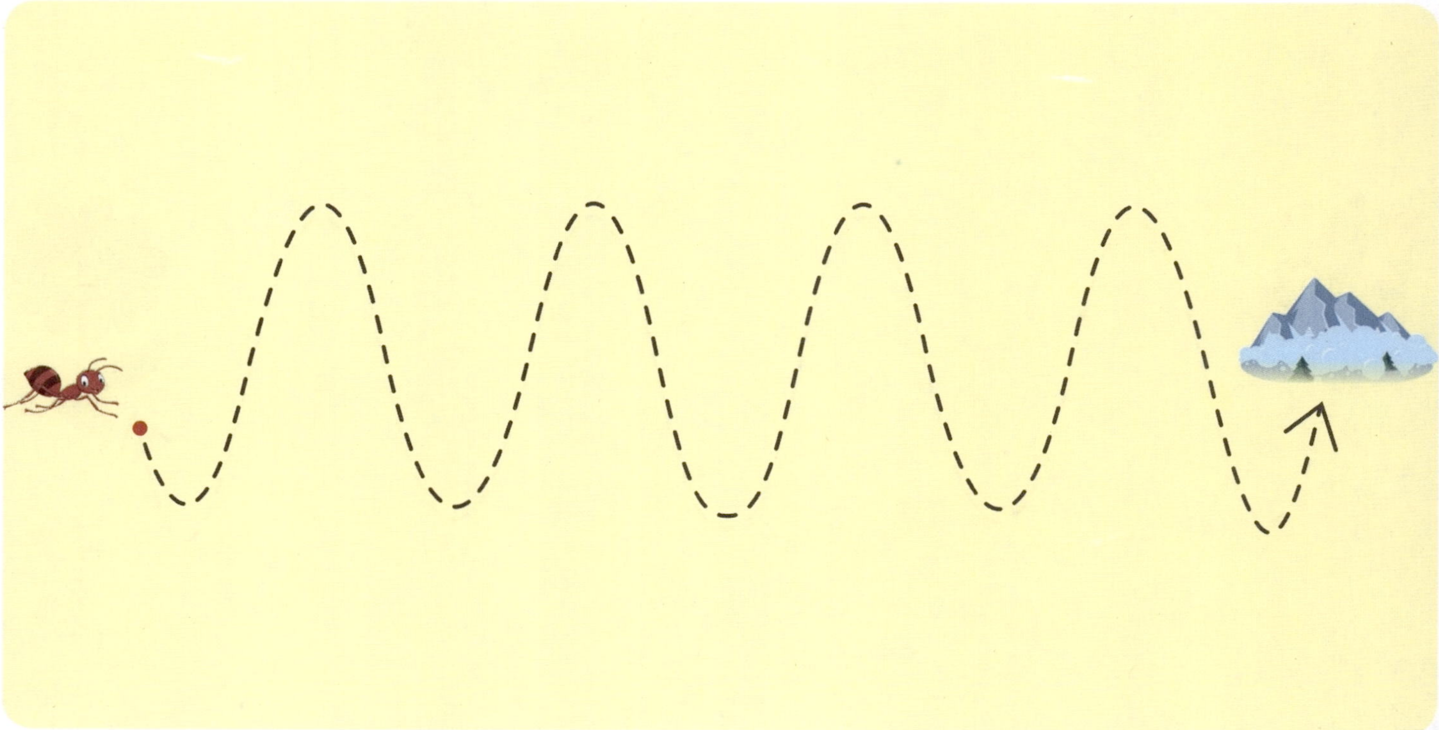

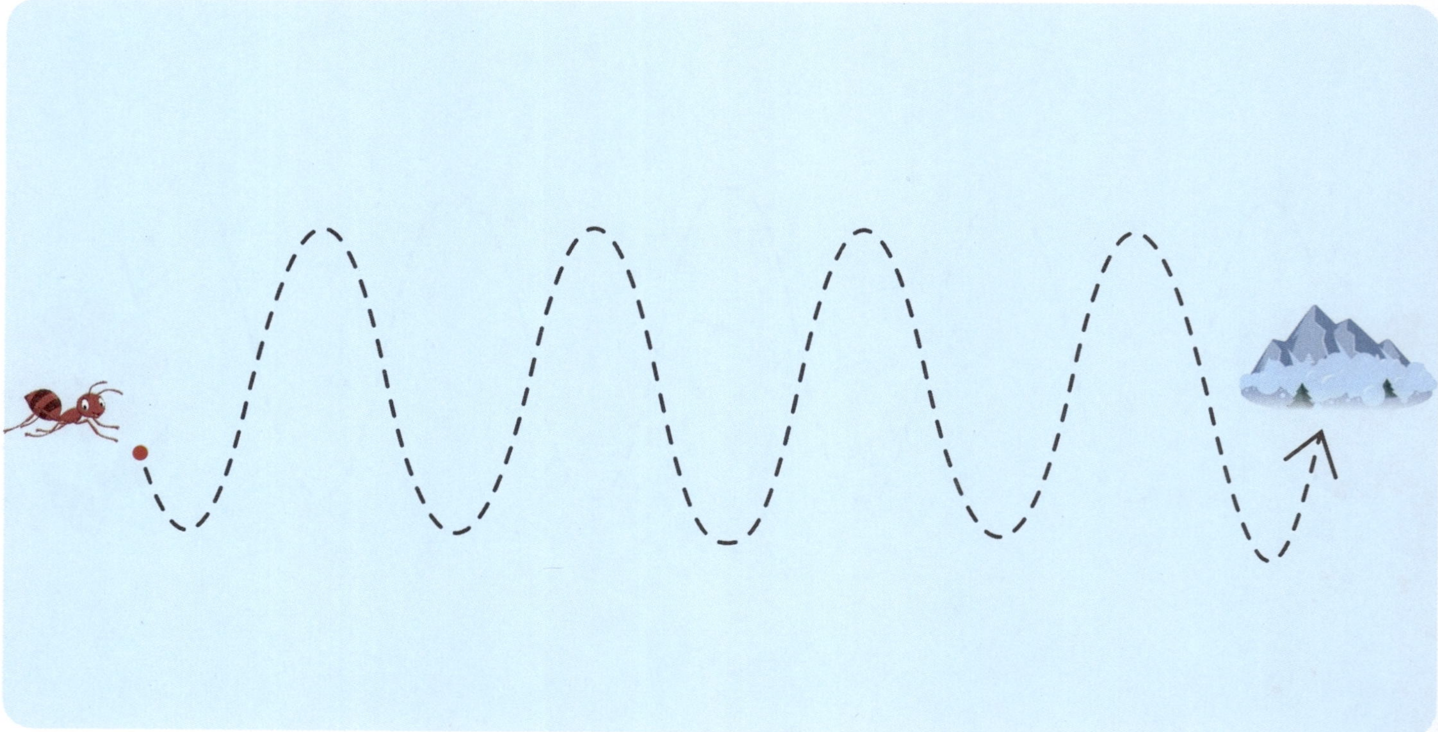

Let's Trace Patterns

Trace the patterns.

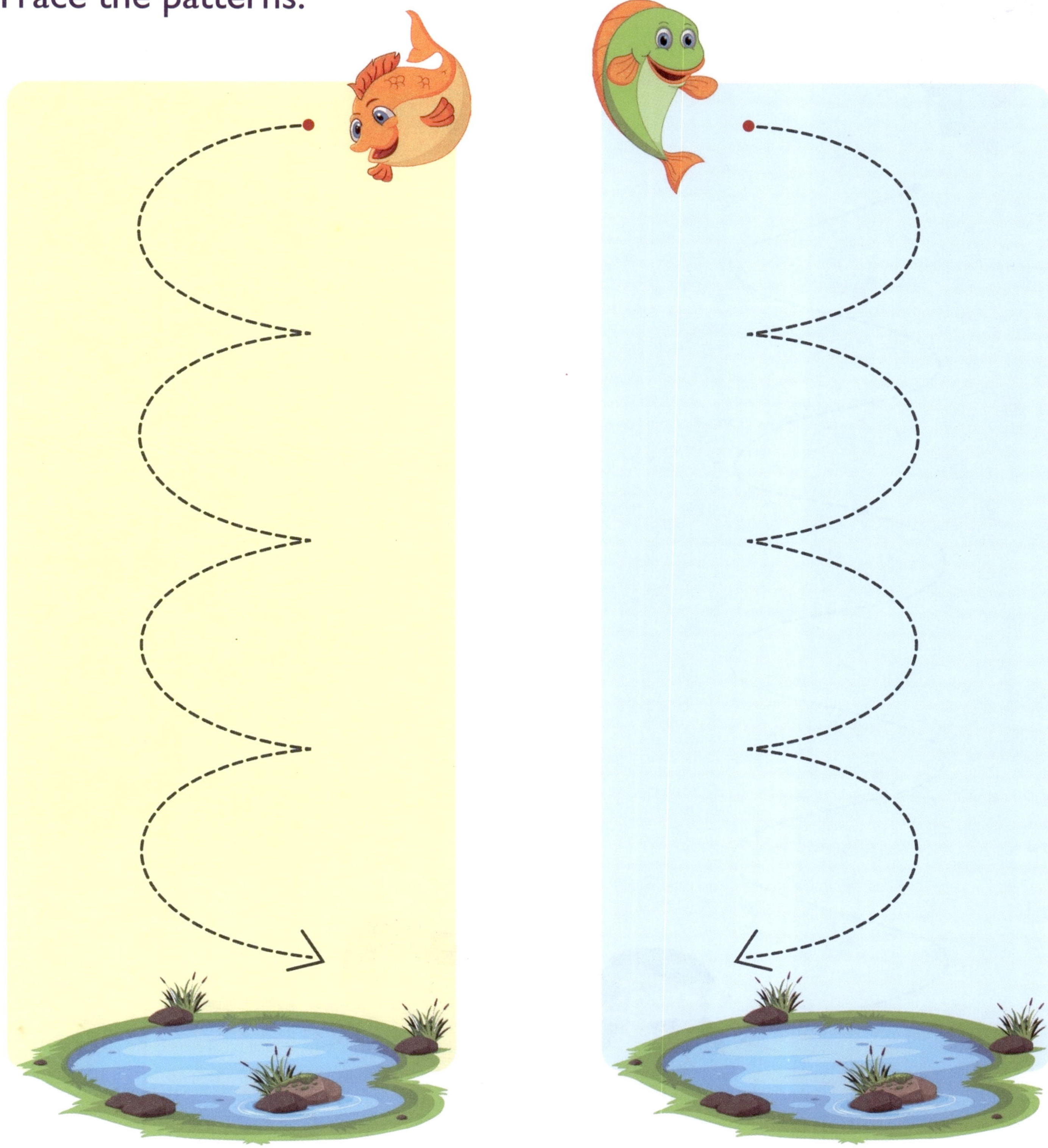

Let's Trace Patterns

Trace the patterns.

Let's Make Loops and Curves

Trace the patterns.

Let's Make Loops and Curves

Trace the patterns.

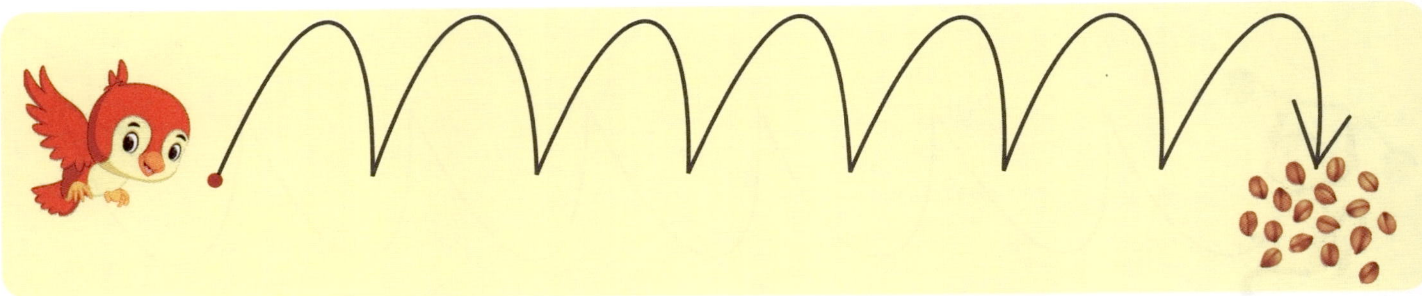

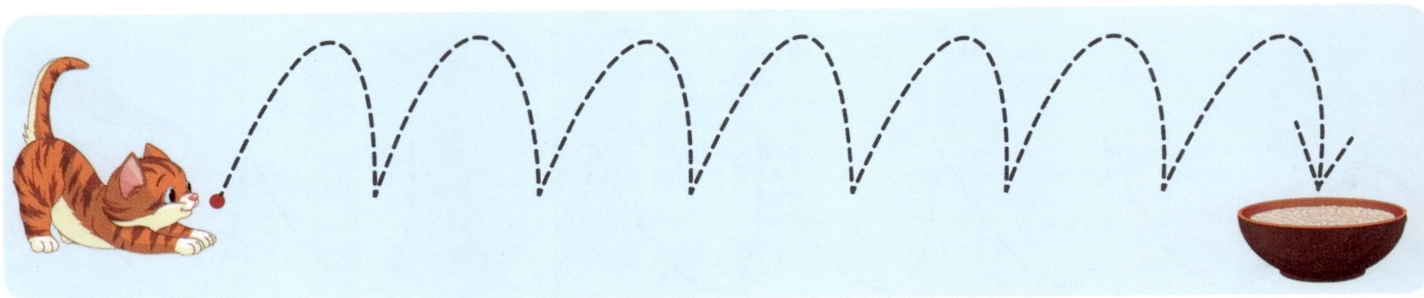

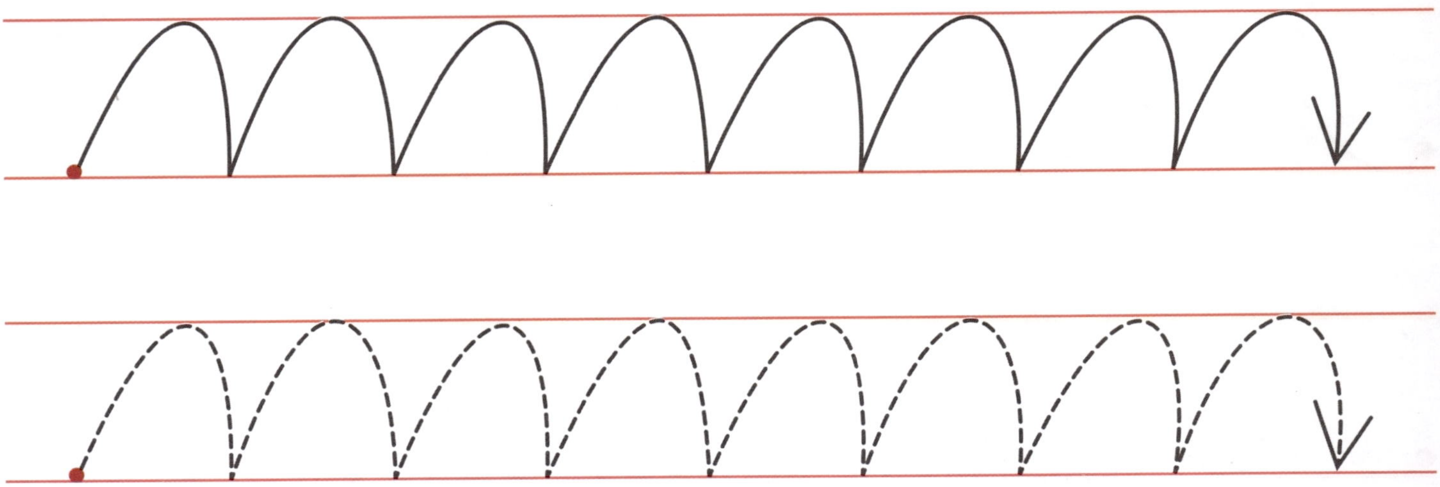

Let's Make Loops and Curves

Trace the patterns.

Let's Make Loops and Curves

Trace the patterns.

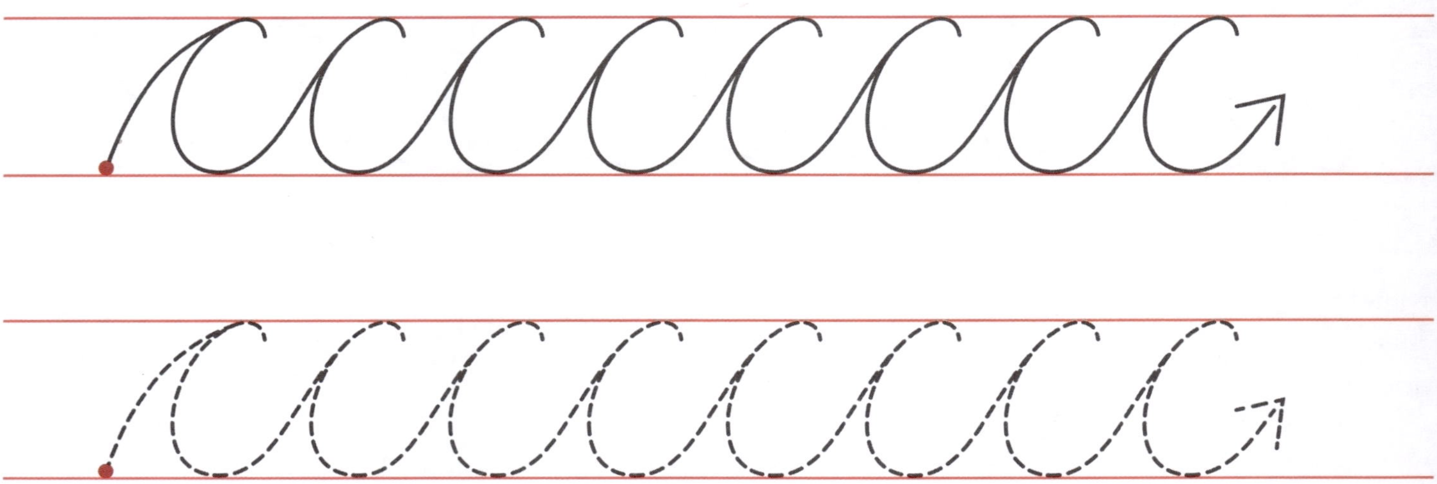

Let's Make Loops and Curves

Trace the patterns.

Let's Trace Letters

Trace with crayons.

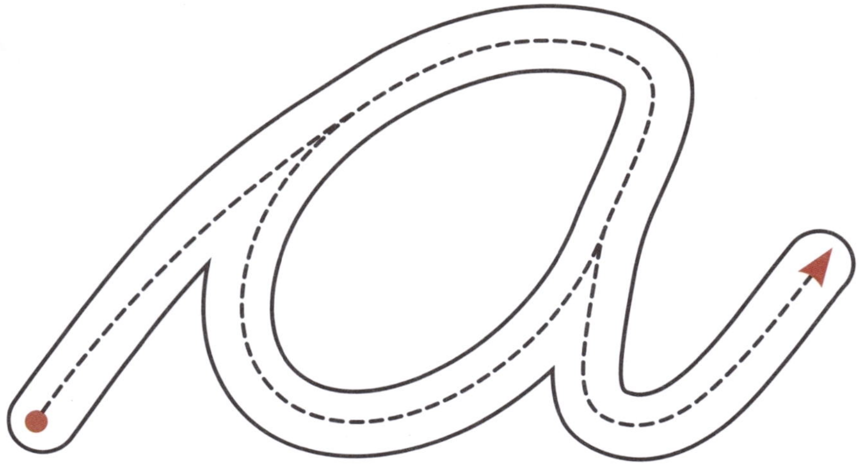

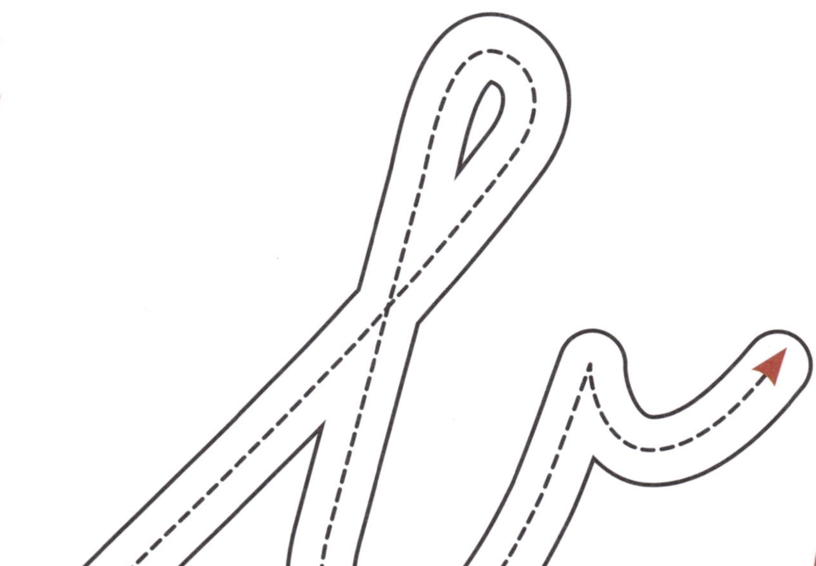

Let's Trace Letters

Trace with crayons.

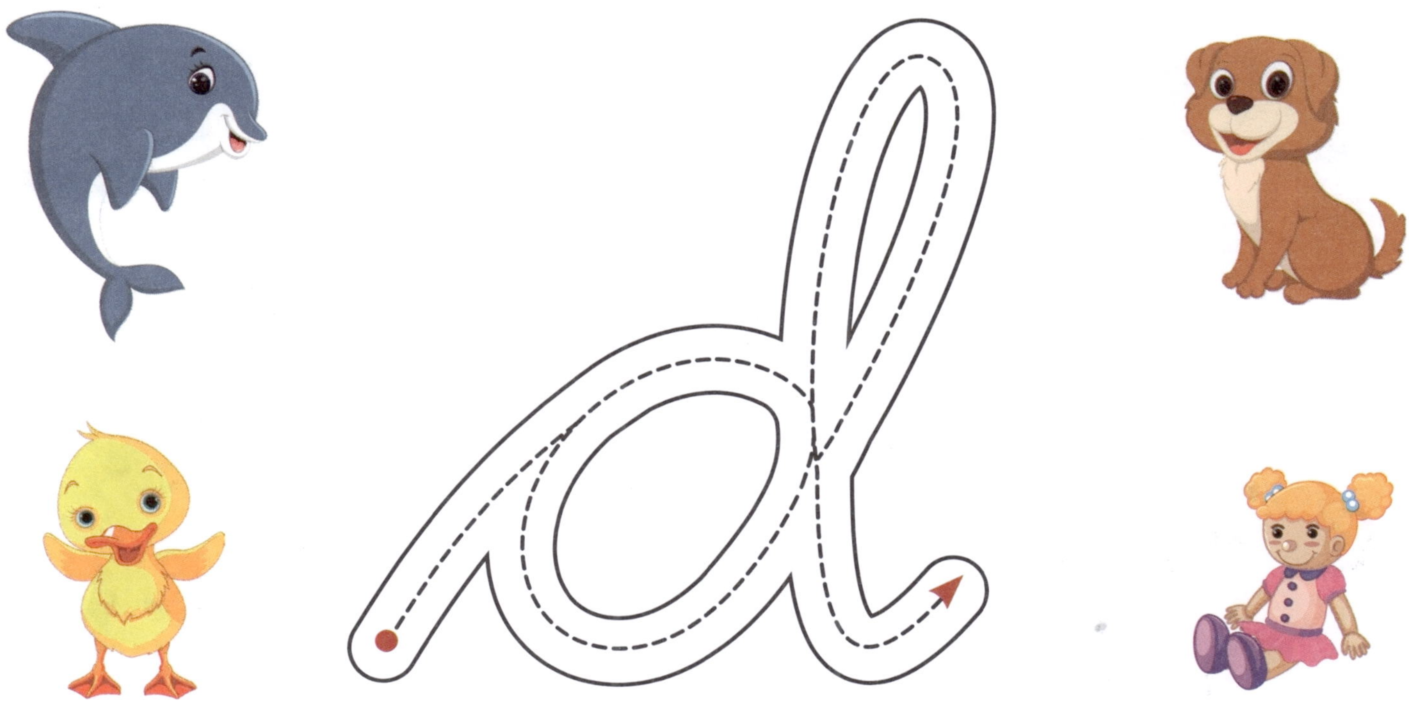

Let's Trace Letters

Trace with crayons.

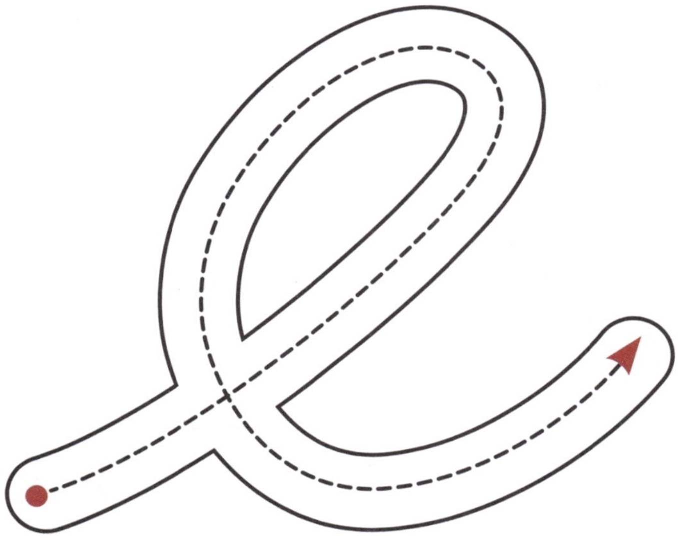

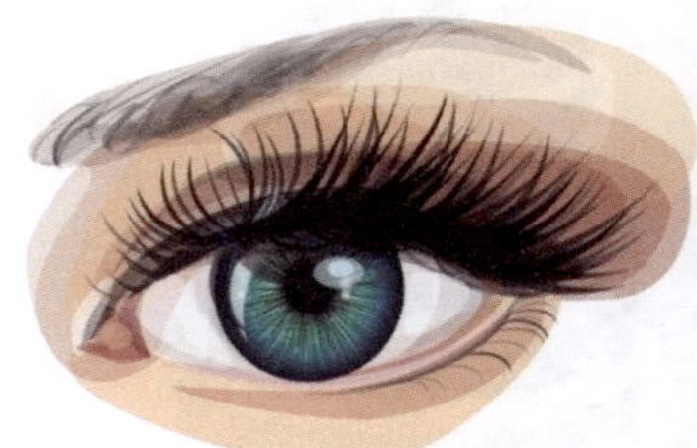

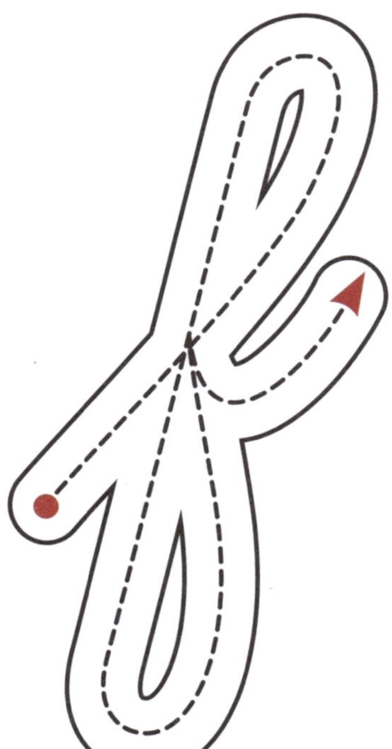

Let's Trace Letters

Trace with crayons.

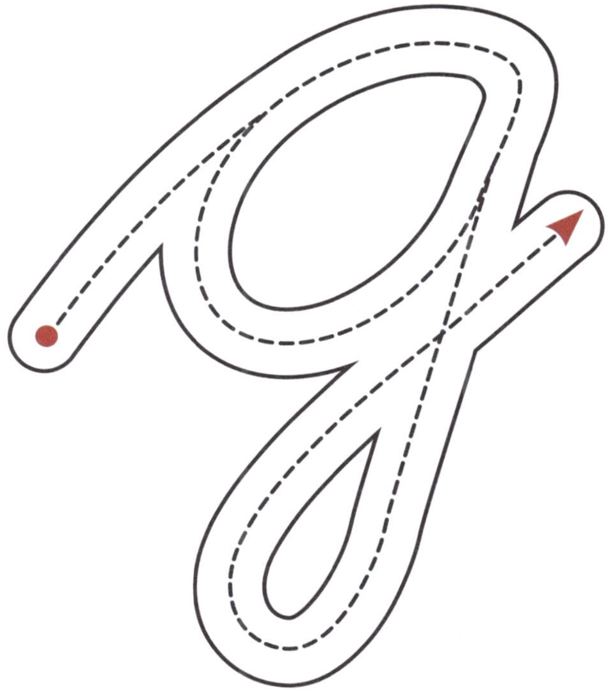

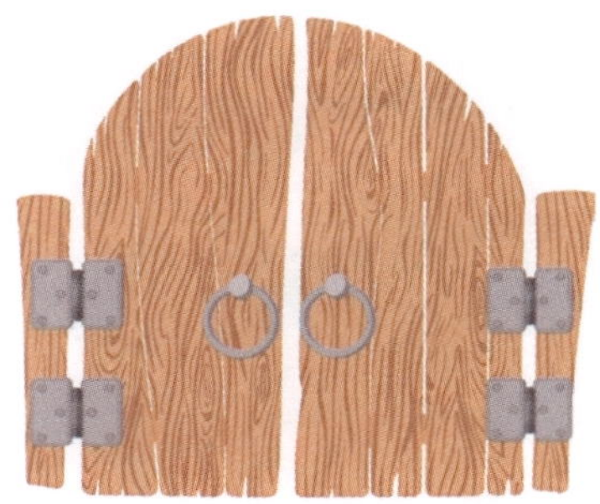

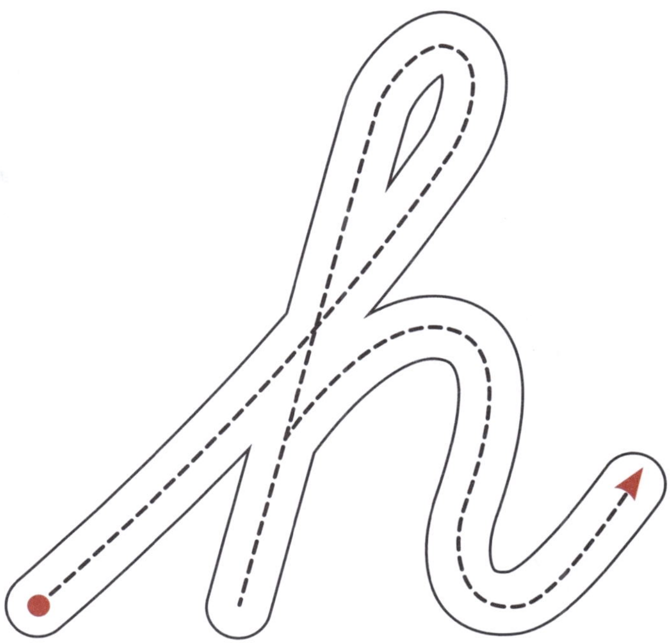

Let's Trace Letters

Trace with crayons.

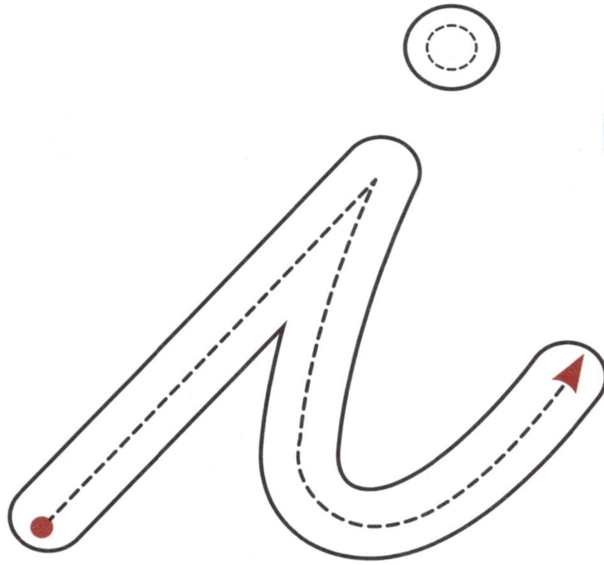

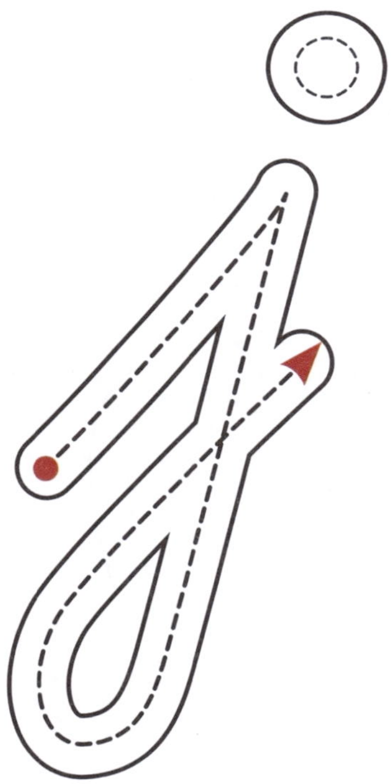

Let's Trace Letters

Trace with crayons.

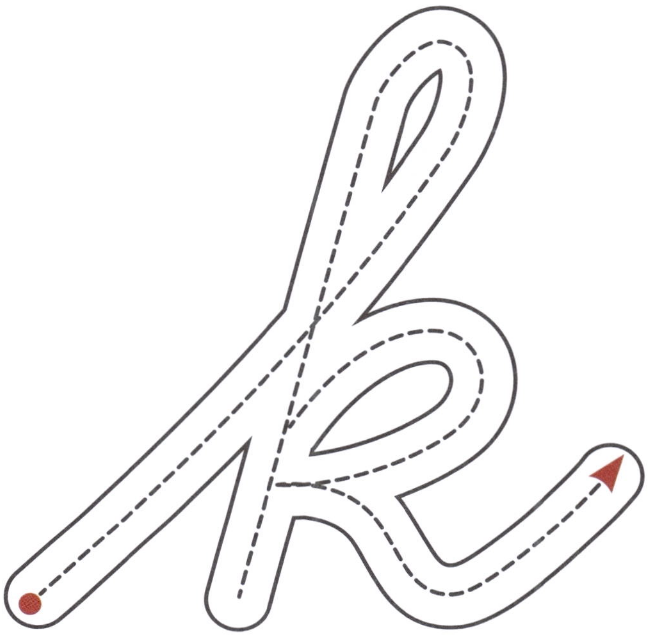

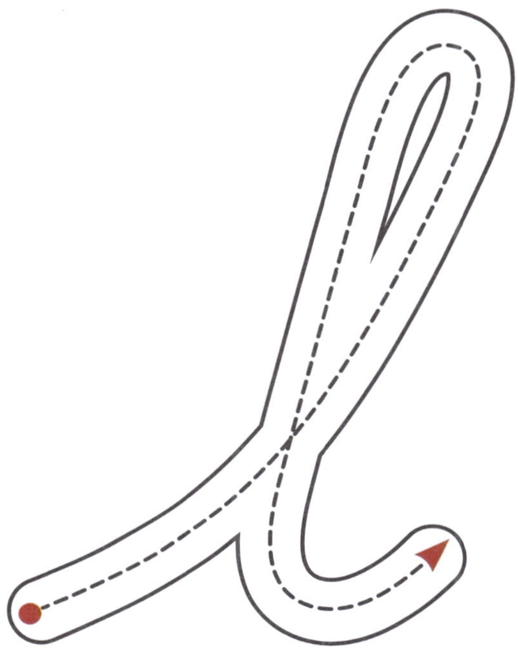

Let's Trace Letters

Trace with crayons.

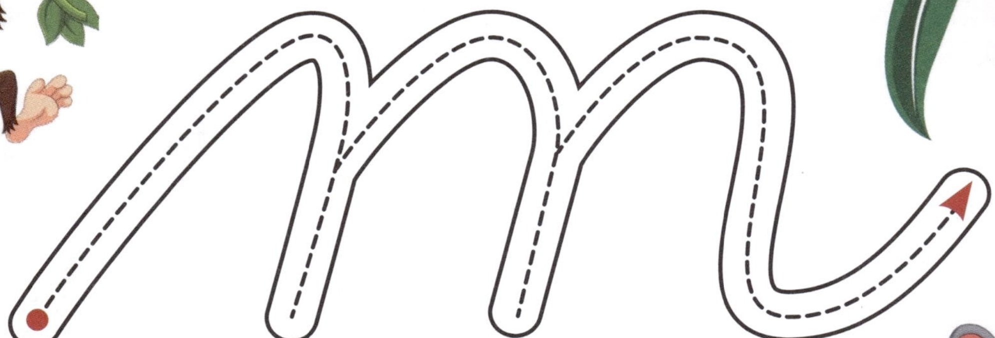

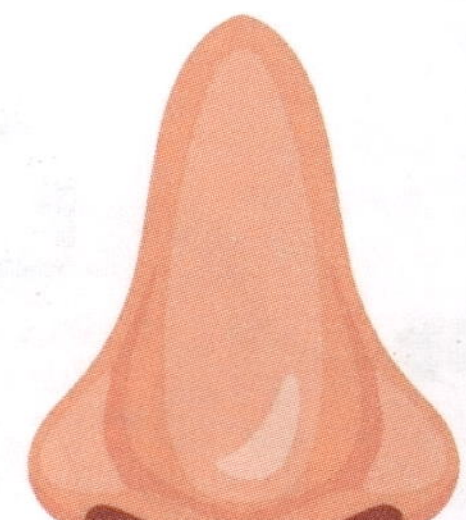

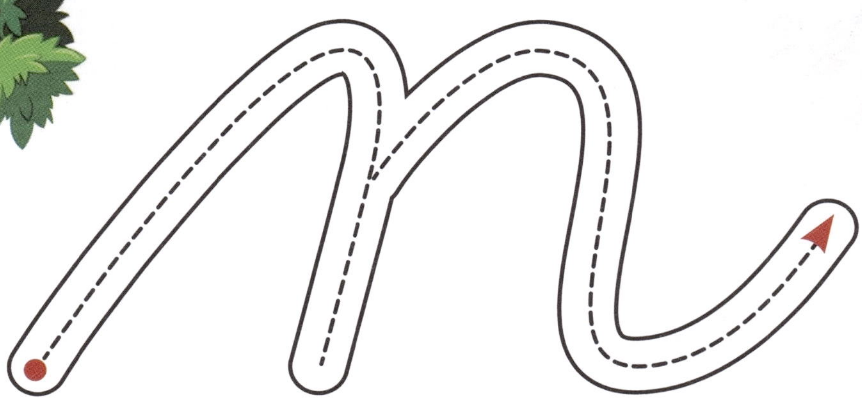

Let's Trace Letters

Trace with crayons.

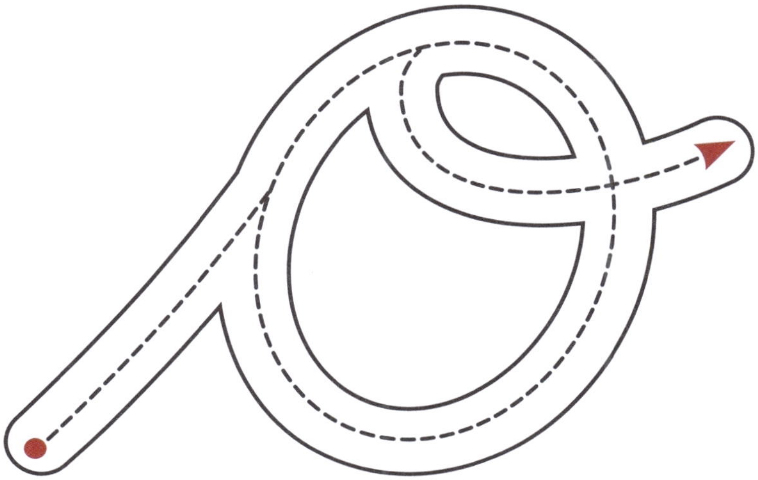

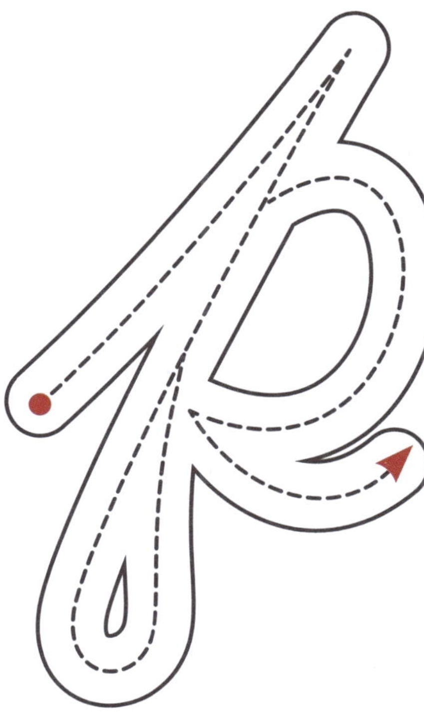

Let's Trace Letters

Trace with crayons.

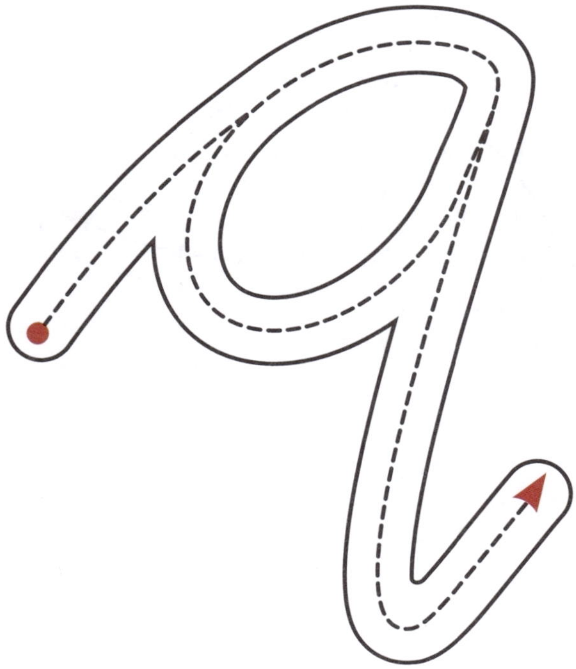

Let's Trace Letters

Trace with crayons.

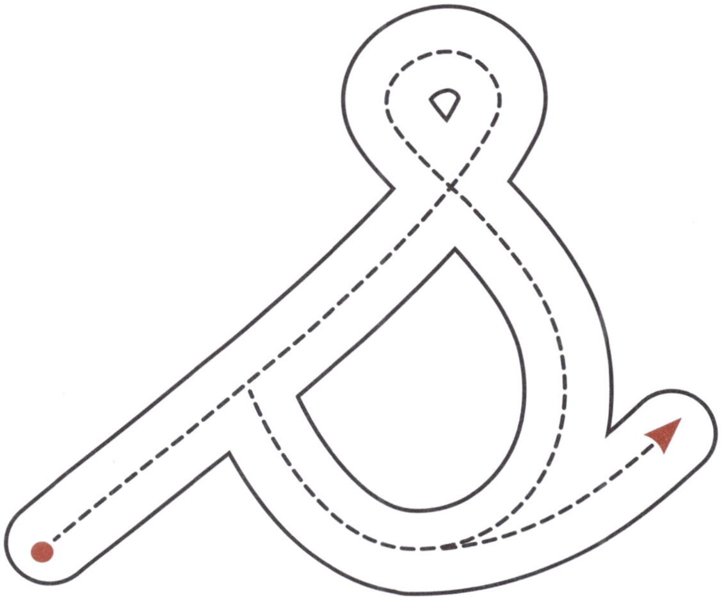

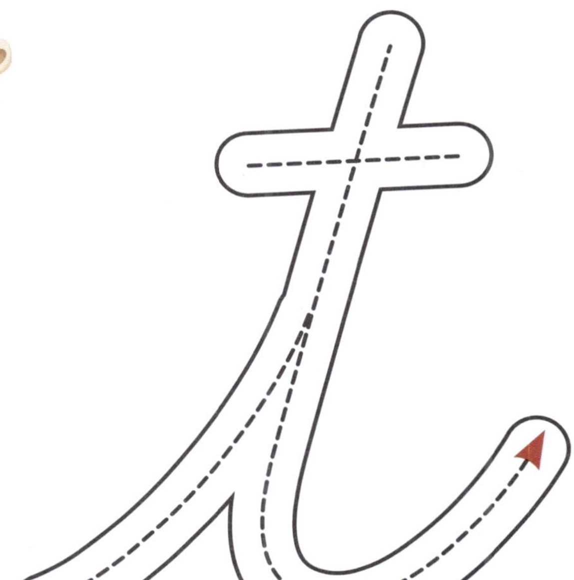

Let's Trace Letters

Trace with crayons.

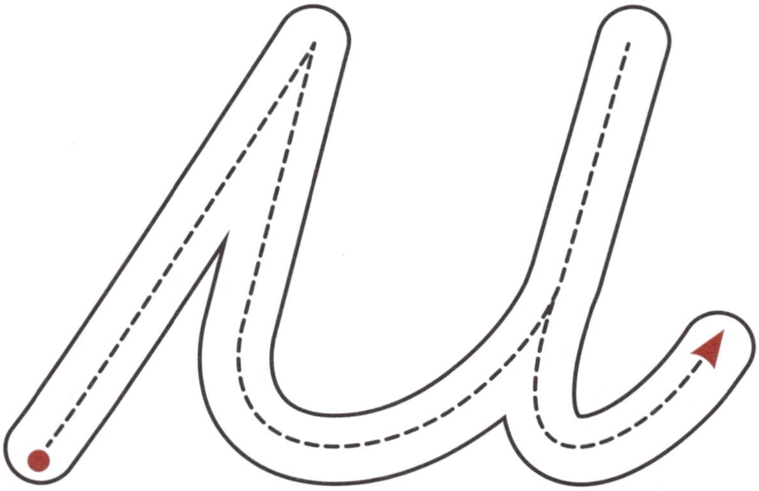

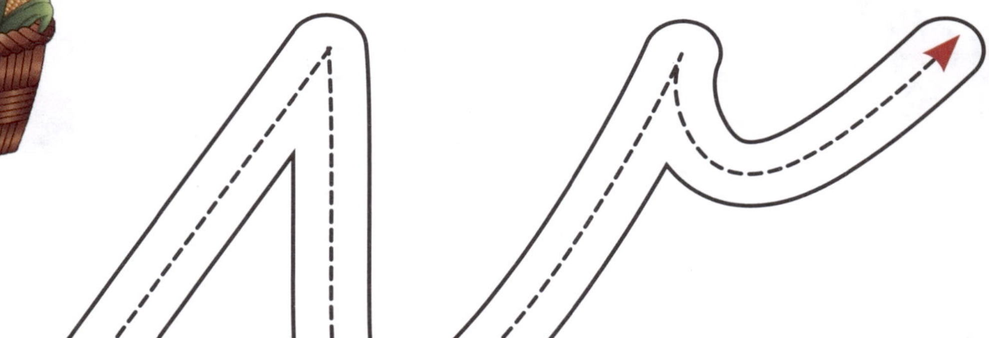

Let's Trace Letters

Trace with crayons.

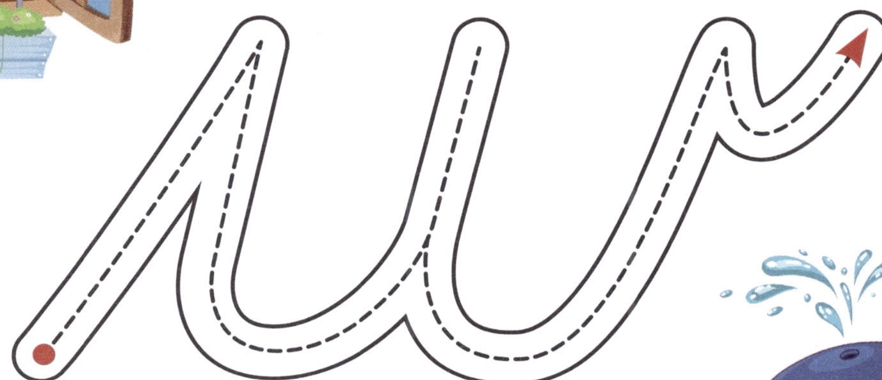

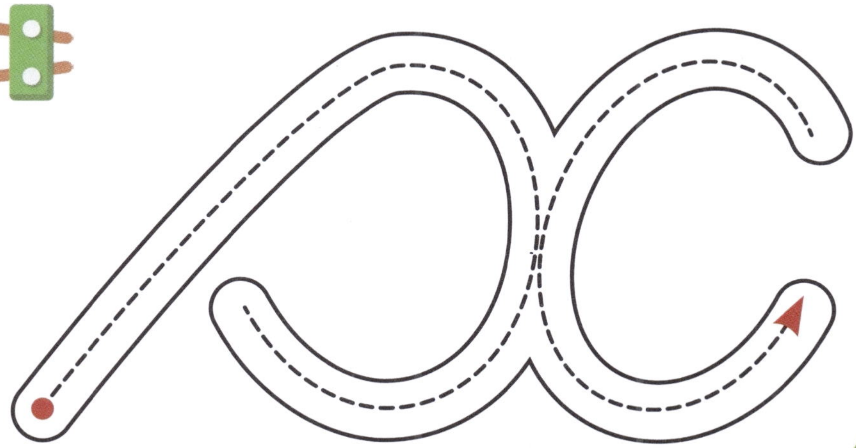

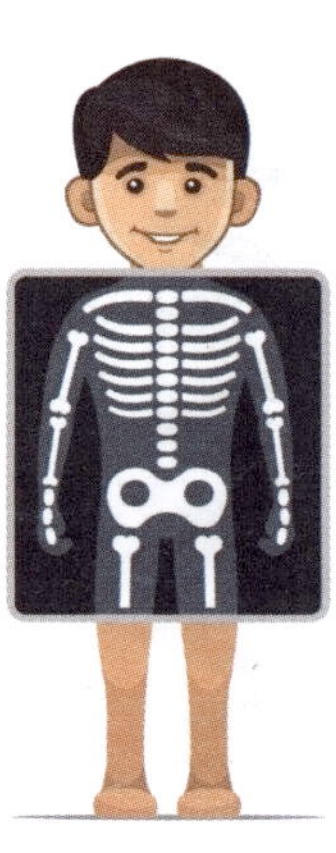

Let's Trace Letters

Trace with crayons.

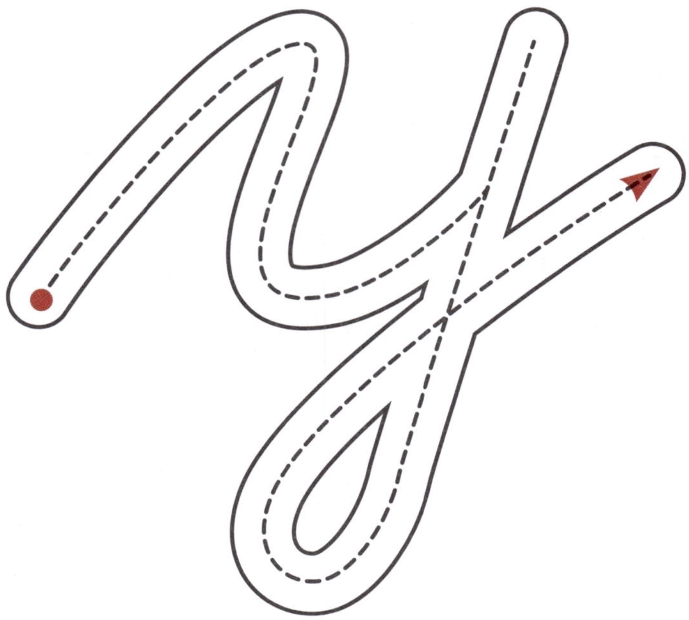

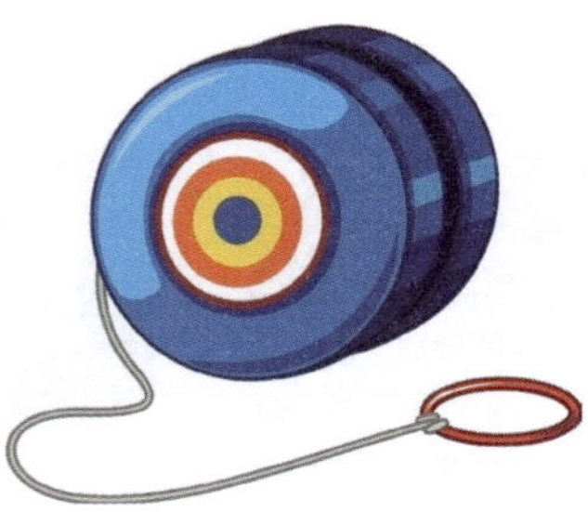

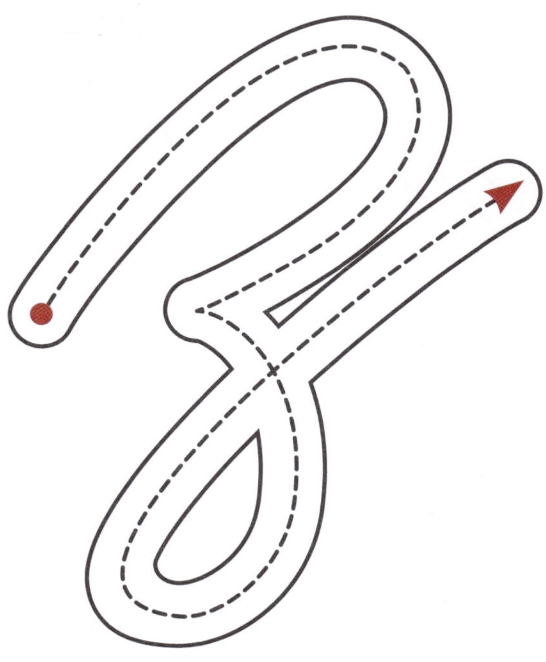